STEP
FORWARD
WITH

RESPONSIBLE
DECISION-MAKING

WE
RECYCLE

SHANNON WELBOURN

Crabtree Publishing Company

www.crabtreebooks.com

STEP FORWARD!

Author
Shannon Welbourn

Series research and development
Reagan Miller

Editorial director
Kathy Middleton

Editors
Reagan Miller, Janine Deschenes

Series Consultant
Larry Miller: BA (Sociology), BPE, MSc.Ed
Retired teacher, guidance counselor, and certified coach

Print and production coordinator
Katherine Berti

Design and photo research
Katherine Berti

Photographs
Alamy: ZUMA Press, Inc.: p 17
Istockphoto: p. 11 (right)
Other images by Shutterstock

Library and Archives Canada Cataloguing in Publication

Welbourn, Shannon, author
    Step forward with responsible decision-making / Shannon
Welbourn.

(Step forward!)
Includes index.
Issued in print and electronic formats.
ISBN 978-0-7787-2769-9 (hardback).--
ISBN 978-0-7787-2820-7 (paperback).--
ISBN 978-1-4271-1827-1 (html)

    1. Decision making--Juvenile literature. I. Title.

BF448.W44 2016   j153.8'3   C2016-903353-8
                                          C2016-903354-6

Library of Congress Cataloging-in-Publication Data

CIP Available at the Library of Congress

Crabtree Publishing Company

www.crabtreebooks.com   1-800-387-7650

Printed in Canada/102016/IH20160811

Published in Canada
Crabtree Publishing
616 Welland Ave.
St. Catharines, Ontario
L2M 5V6

Published in the United States
Crabtree Publishing
PMB 59051
350 Fifth Avenue, 59th Floor
New York, New York 10118

Published in the United Kingdom
Crabtree Publishing
Maritime House
Basin Road North, Hove
BN41 1WR

Published in Australia
Crabtree Publishing
3 Charles Street
Coburg North
VIC 3058

CONTENTS

WHAT IS RESPONSIBLE DECISION-MAKING?

We make choices every day. Our choices make us the people we are.

Some of our choices, or decisions, are easy to make and take little time. Choosing which pair of socks to wear to school is a decision we can make in seconds. Other decisions take more time and thought to make. These require us to practice responsible decision-making. Responsible decision-making means thinking about the **outcomes** of our decisions before making them. How will your choices affect you and others? When you make responsible decisions with others in mind, people will learn they can depend on you to **respect** others.

When you make decisions, you have to decide what is right and wrong.

COMPUTER GAME

SCHOOL

TOY STORE

FUTURE

AMUSEMENT

PLAYGROUND

WHY DO OUR DECISIONS MATTER?

We make decisions based on what we believe is right and what is expected of us, such as sharing with others and taking turns.

Choices make us who we are. This is why it is so important to make responsible choices. Responsible decision-making is a skill you will use throughout your life. The decisions you make can have different outcomes. They can be **positive** or **negative**.

When you make an **agreement** with someone, they need to know that they can trust you to uphold your agreement. If you don't keep your agreement, there may be **consequences**. Other people will be disappointed. You could be disappointed with yourself because you let down others. When you keep your promises, you show others that you are able to make responsible decisions.

We can't see into the future, but practicing responsible decision-making can help us predict outcomes of our actions.

STEPS TO RESPONSIBLE DECISION-MAKING

The steps outlined below help to guide you through the decision-making process. The steps can be used to make decisions about school, friends, and other areas in your life.

1

Identify the choice that you need to make.

2

Identify possible decisions you might make.

3

Brainstorm outcomes for each possible decision.

4 Decide whether your decisions are responsible. Ask yourself:

- Do my decisions support my **goals**?

- Are my decisions based on what is best for me, or am I allowing other people or things to affect my decisions?

5 Choose the most responsible decision—the one that is best for you and fits your goals.

6 Reflect, or think back, about the outcome.

- Was the outcome of your decision positive or negative? How do you know?

- Would you change your decision?

RESPONSIBLE DECISION-MAKING AT SCHOOL

Community

School   Home

Each day at school, you have an opportunity to make choices and learn from them.

You aren't the only student in your class! At school, you have to think about how your decisions affect your classmates. For example, when working on a project as a group, everyone is expected to do their part. You might be working on homework for your group project when a friend asks you to play road hockey. You really want to play, but you know you will be letting down your group if you don't finish your work. Responsible decision-making means you think about how your choices will affect others.

12

What are the outcomes if you choose to play hockey? How do they affect others?

Sometimes, the hardest decisions are when we choose between doing what is right and doing what will be fun in the moment.

RESPONSIBLE DECISION-MAKING IN YOUR COMMUNITY

A community is a group of people who live, work, and play in a place. Your home, school, and neighborhood are part of your community.

Responsible decision-making is a skill you use every place you go. Many kids are part of clubs and sports teams. Responsible decision-making is just as important in clubs and sports teams as it is at home and school. Your choices should show respect for others. You and your friends are part of a soccer team. A friend suggests skipping practice one day to play video games at her house. You know that playing video games will be a lot of fun, but you also wonder about the outcomes of choosing to skip practice.

You stop and think about what could happen.

Positive outcomes
• have fun
• try out new video game

Negative outcomes
• my parents won't know where I am
• my coach will be upset
• my teammates will be disappointed

STEP FURTHER

Can you add any other outcomes to the list? What would be your next step to make a decision?

XIUHTEZCATL MARTINEZ

Xiuhtezcatl (shu-tez-cat) Martinez is an environmental activist. **This means he works very hard to protect the environment where he lives.**

At the early age of six, Xiuhtezcatl noticed that the forest near his home was changing. Fires were happening often and trees were dying. He could no longer see the plants and animals that lived there. He knew people had to make responsible decisions to save the forest. He decided to speak up.

10:44 AM

Name: Xiuhtezcatl Martinez

From: Boulder, Colorado

Accomplishment: Protects the environment and helps others make good decisions.

Xiuhtezcatl made a brave choice. He spoke in front of a crowd at a meeting in his town. He encouraged his community to make responsible decisions to save the environment. He did not stop until he was heard. Ten years later, Xiuhtezcatl shares his message around the world. He has helped other young people decide to speak up. We are all responsible for making good decisions to protect Earth. The decisions we make now will have long-term effects on the environment.

"This generation gets to decide what kind of world future generations will live in forever. I believe we have the power to turn things around. It's really our responsibility."

—Xiuhtezcatl Martinez

OVERCOMING CHALLENGES

It's not always easy to make responsible decisions. It is a skill that you will get better at over time.

It can be difficult to make responsible decisions because people may not always agree with your choices. You have to believe that you are doing the right thing. For example, if you saw a boy being picked on by others at school, a responsible decision would be to stand up for him. You are choosing to do what you think is right, even though others don't agree.

Sometimes, making the right decision means that you are going against what others think.

These questions can help guide you toward making responsible decisions:

- How will my decision affect others?
- Does my decision fit what's best for me, or am I letting others decide for me?
- What are the possible outcomes of my decision? What could go right or wrong?
- Have I made a past decision that could help me make the right choice now?

ENCOURAGING OTHERS

Your choices can have a positive effect on others, too. When you make responsible decisions, others can learn from them.

A **role model** is a person who acts in a way that others respect. By making good decisions, you can be a role model. You act like a role model when you:

- are a good listener;
- share what you've learned from your past decision-making;
- help friends brainstorm choices and outcomes
- respect your friends' ideas, and don't pressure them to agree with you.

Can you tell me more about the choice you have to make?

Help please!

Try my idea!

Talking to friends and family can be helpful when making tough decisions.

I know how you feel. I've been there before and learned from my experience. Let's work through this together.

Let's brainstorm some more choices and outcomes!

That choice might have a negative outcome.

My opinion is different, but I respect your choice.

STEP FURTHER

What other ways can you be a role model for friends who have choices to make?

STEPPING FORWARD

Responsible decision-making is a skill that helps you make choices that have positive outcomes. You will use it throughout your life.

This list describes some important responsible decision-making habits. Review this list again and again in the future to make sure you keep stepping forward with responsible decision-making!

On a separate piece of paper, write down yes or no after reading each statement. How are you already making responsible decisions? In what ways could you help improve your decision-making skills?

1) I look back at outcomes from my past decisions to help me learn and improve. **YES** NO

2) I resist making choices that get me what I want now if they may lead to problems later. **YES** NO

3) I take responsibility for the positive and negative outcomes of my choices. YES **NO**

4) I always make choices that follow what I believe is right. **YES** NO

LEARNING MORE

BOOKS

Javernick, Ellen. *What If Everybody Did That?*
Marshall Cavendish, 2010.

Aloian, Molly. *Live it: Responsibility.*
Crabtree Publishing, 2010.

Burstein, John. *I Said No! Refusal Skills.*
Crabtree Publishing, 2010.

WEBSITES

www.earthguardians.org/xiuhtezcatl
Learn about Xiuhtezcatl Martinez's story and mission at the website for his organization, Earth Guardians.

**http://tedxtalks.ted.com/video/
The-Global-Crisis-and-the-Power**
Listen to Xiuhtezcatl speak his message, empowering youth to make the choice to save the environment.

http://bit.ly/1Wgaryc
Visit this site to learn some decision-making tips from real kids!

WORDS TO KNOW

activist [ak-tuh-vist] noun A person who speaks up for a cause

agreement [uh-gree-muhnt] noun An accepted plan between two or more people

consequences [kon-si-kwens] noun Result or outcome of a previous decision

expectation [ek-spek-TEY-sh*uh*n] noun An action that is expected, or anticipated, of someone

goals [gohls] noun The aim toward which effort is directed

negative [neg-uh-tiv] adjective Lacking positive qualities

outcomes [OUT-kuhms] noun The results of an action or process

positive [POZ-i-tiv] adjective Describing something with an agreeable or favorable effect

respect [ri-SPEKT] noun The act of giving something or someone the attention it deserves

responsible [ri-spon-suh-buhl] adjective Reliable or dependable

role model [rohl MOD-l] noun A person who is respected by others

INDEX

ABOUT THE AUTHOR

Shannon Welbourn is a freelance author of educational K-12 books. She holds an honors BA in Child & Youth Studies, and is a certified teacher. Shannon works full-time as a Library and Media Specialist. In this position, she works closely with teachers and teacher candidates, helping to inspire and develop a passion for learning. Shannon lives close to Niagara Falls and enjoys vacationing in the Muskokas with her family.